Everything You Need to Know About
PEER
MEDIATION

Peer mediation offers students a peaceful solution to resolving
conflicts.

Everything You Need to Know About

PEER MEDIATION

Nancy N. Rue

THE ROSEN PUBLISHING GROUP, INC.
NEW YORK

Published in 1997 by The Rosen Publishing Group, Inc.
29 East 21st Street, New York, NY 10010

First Edition

Manufactured in the United States of America

Library of Congress Cataloging-in-Publication Data

Rue, Nancy N.
    Everything you need to know about peer mediation / by Nancy N. Rue.
       p.   cm.
    Includes bibliographical references and index.
    Summary: Explains the principles of peer mediation and advises on how to
participate in or start such a program as a way to manage conflict and
resolve problems.
    ISBN 0-8239-2435-1 (lib. binding)
    1. Mediation—Juvenile literature.   2. Negotiation—Juvenile literature.
3. Conflict management—Juvenile literature.   4. Peer counseling of students—Juvenile literature. [1. Negotiation. 2. Conflict management.
3. Problem solving.]   I. Title.
    BF637.M4R84 1996
    303.6′9—dc20   90-34712
                                               CIP
                                              AC

Contents

Introduction   6

1. What Is Peer Mediation?   11

2. The Rules of the Game   18

3. Choosing Peer Mediation   32

4. Peer Mediators in Training   39

5. Valuable Skills   51

   Glossary—*Explaining New Words*   59

   Where to Go for Help   61

   For Further Reading   62

   Index   63

Introduction

*J*ustin was angry at Thad for picking on his sister, Cassandra. At the end of gym class, hidden behind a row of lockers, he waited for Thad. When Thad walked by, Justin tripped him. Thad fell on the floor and Justin said, "Let that remind you to stay away from my sister."

The rest of the students gathered around to watch. Thad felt embarrassed, surprised, and angry.

As Justin turned around to leave, Thad stood up. "You can't make me!" he shouted, facing Justin and tossing his books aside.

Justin took a step forward and said, "I think I can . . . ."

The ending to this situation may be familiar to many students. Justin shoves Thad; Thad shoves Justin; a fight soon erupts. Both students are then either sent home or to detention. And, worst of all, the original conflict between Thad and Justin is never resolved.

However, the ending could be different if Justin and Thad had known about peer mediation. Peer mediation is part of a larger movement to reduce violence in schools by teaching students to solve conflicts peaceably through a process called conflict resolution.

There are three different ways that conflict resolution programs can work in a school.

1. Train teachers to use conflict resolution in their classrooms to help their students solve problems with each other.
2. Offer conflict resolution as an academic subject, like math or English.
3. Teach students in the school how to mediate when problems arise between students.

Although we will only be talking about the third method in this book, it's important to remember that the most successful programs include all three areas of conflict resolution.

Many young people think that they have no control over violence in their school and home that comes from conflict. They feel helpless. But those involved in the conflict resolution movement know that violence doesn't have to happen, *especially* in the schools. They believe in a "new way of fighting" that can help solve conflict before it leads to violence. At the same time, conflict resolution gives students the power to choose solutions other than violence.

In this book you will learn what peer mediation

Peer mediation is being used to successfully lower the violence rate
in schools.

is and how it works. You will read about many schools across the country that have successfully used peer mediation programs to lower the amount of violence between students. You will also find out about the many ways to be involved with your peer mediation program. If your school does not have a peer mediation program, you will learn the steps involved in starting one.

The skills you learn in peer mediation extend far beyond the classroom. You will hear from actual peer mediators about the lessons they have learned and how it has affected their lives—both in and out of school.

Conflict is a part of life, but it does not have to end in violence.

Chapter 1

What Is Peer Mediation?

Conflict is part of life. Human beings are never going to agree on everything all the time. Conflict gives people a chance to grow and a chance to see and appreciate their differences. Conflict can actually help dissolve prejudice. The important thing is that conflict should not turn into violence.

Unfortunately, conflicts usually come to a point where people feel that their only choices are to fight or walk away. Many people feel that the only way to end a conflict and maintain their pride is through fighting. Few people want to fight, and yet most want to stand up for themselves and express their anger.

Young people in peer mediation programs find other solutions. In the mediation sessions, with the help of the mediators, they search for creative, nonviolent solutions to their conflicts. In this way students try to settle their conflict so that neither person is left feeling angry or hurt. The idea is that people can learn the necessary skills to find a peaceful solution to conflict.

The most important part of the peer mediation process is honest communication. Without both people actively listening to each other, a peaceful solution is almost impossible. You can learn to say how you feel instead of acting out in a violent way. You can learn how to communicate your needs while working to meet the needs of the other as well. Peer mediation programs show you how to do that by guiding you through problem situations when they arise.

Through peer mediation, students learn how to create a "peaceable school," a safe place where they can try peaceful methods of resolving conflicts before they become violent. Students in these schools have a different sense of their world. They see a future full of hope that no one will be afraid to face.

How It Came About

The seeds for conflict resolution methods were planted in the 1960s during the peace movement. At that time, new ways were being sought to solve problems without physical and verbal force. But the methods were only put into use in the schools in the late 1980s—in response to the rise in violence among students.

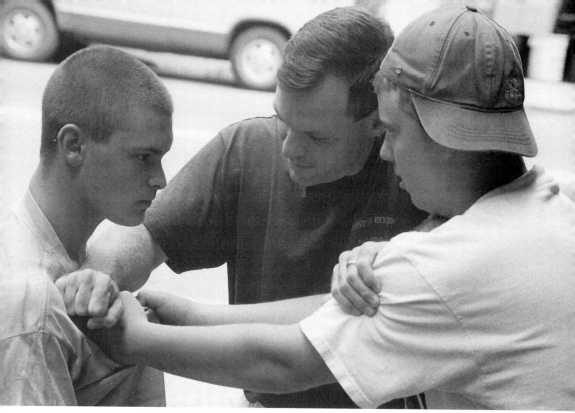

It can be difficult to concentrate in school when you are surrounded by violence.

Many violent crimes are happening in a place that used to be considered safe—school. Some studies have shown that the risk of violence to teenagers is greater in school than anywhere else. The Department of Justice says that each day 100,000 young people carry guns to school. Each hour, more than 2,000 students are physically attacked on school grounds. More than 400,000 violent crimes are reported in and around U.S. schools each year. In a study of eighth and tenth grade students, 34 percent said that someone had threatened to hurt them during the year.

There are several reasons why peer mediation works so well. They include:

1. No "authority figures" force students to accept their solutions. The people involved in the conflict make the decisions themselves. They create and own the solution.
2. It does more than solve the problem, it teaches the people involved how to solve future ones. It offers them a chance to learn a new skill that will be useful throughout their lives.
3. Conflicts will usually dissolve if they are settled by the people involved in the conflict. Mediation offers a safe, isolated environment.
4. Mediation gives students a way to get rid of their anger *and* solve the problem.
5. It's a very formal process. The structure and safety of the mediation process often helps calm people's emotions and lower the anxiety.
6. It can work for a wide range of disputes. The mediators give *every* conflict equal importance.

Let's look at a possible ending to Justin and Thad's argument. With the use of peer mediation, it might go something like this:

Justin took a step toward Thad, fists raised. Just then the gym teacher stepped between them and presented two options: detention or peer mediation. Neither student could afford another detention so they agreed to try peer mediation.

They set up an appointment and met the following day during lunch in the mediation room. The mediation room was an area set aside by the school where students could go to resolve conflicts, with the help of the mediators. They found several comfortable chairs and a refrigerator. Nick, one of the two mediators, offered both Thad and Justin a cola.

"Before we begin," Denise, the other mediator said, "you both have to agree to a few rules. First, you have to agree that you want to solve the problem, or it won't work."

Justin shrugged, "Sure."

Thad leaned back in his chair. "I want to settle it without getting my teeth knocked out, so, yeah, I agree."

"Second," Nick said, "you have to settle this without name-calling and without interrupting each other." Both Thad and Justin agreed.

Justin and Thad sat across from each other at the mediation table. Justin spoke first. He told his side of the story, explaining his fear and anger for the way Thad was treating his sister. Thad then was given a chance to tell his side of the situation.

"Okay, Justin," Nick said when they were finished, "now that you've heard Thad's side, what could you have done differently to keep this whole thing from getting this far?"

Justin looked down, "I could have talked to my sister after she had calmed down and not right after they had broken up. I should have remembered that she goes overboard sometimes. I should have talked to her again when she was more cool, before threatening Thad."

"What about you, Thad?" Denise said.

"I guess I could have explained my side when he tripped me." Thad frowned. "But what are we supposed to do about it now?"

"That's up to you to decide," Nick said. "And we're here to help. What could you do—right now—Justin, to help solve the problem?"

"I could say this is between him and her, and as long as he doesn't hurt her, that it's none of my business. I feel like it's just a normal break-up now that I've heard his side of the story."

"So you just want to make sure she isn't being hurt," Nick said.

"Right," Justin said.

The questions and answers continued, with Justin giving his suggestions for ways to improve the situation. Denise and Nick clarified the statements to make sure both sides understood. When the bell rang for the end of lunch, Nick reviewed the solution.

"Tonight, Thad, Justin, and Cassandra are going to meet for dinner. Justin will help Cassandra feel safe so she can be honest with Thad. And Thad can explain how he feels. Thad will listen and agree not to call her anymore. Justin has agreed not to threaten Thad or yell at him for anything that's already happened."

Denise handed Justin and Thad a pen. "Sign if you agree," she said.

Reaching a solution to Thad and Justin's problem in this way may seem unlikely to you. But

Through peer mediation, students are able to find peaceful solutions to their conflicts.

hundreds of thousands of students are doing just that in over 200 high schools, middle schools, and even elementary schools across the country.

Schools that support these peer mediation programs report at least ten successful mediations each month. Agreements are reached about 90 percent of the time, and 80 percent of those agreements are kept. Most important, violence in those schools has decreased by at least 10 percent.

Students and teachers say the peer mediation program changes the climate of the school, creating both a positive and a safe place in which to learn.

Chapter 2

The Rules of the Game

*D*evon: *I hear you've been saying things behind my back. Do you deny it?*

Muriel: What difference does it make if I do? You're so full of yourself, you wouldn't believe me anyway.

Devon: Only because I know you're lying!

Muriel: I haven't said anything that isn't true.

Devon: Well, if you're so honest, why did I have to hear it from someone else?

Muriel: I didn't think you could take it!

From this conversation, it sounds like Muriel and Devon want to fight. But according to such groups as Educators for Social Responsibility and the National Association for Mediation in Education (NAME), people (not just kids!) often resort to physical violence only because it's easier than working things out, or because they don't know how to express themselves when they're angry. In spite of the bloody noses and broken bones that result from fighting, it is often much harder for people to figure out how to otherwise approach a problem. It isn't that they don't want to solve it—they just lack the skills. A peer mediation program can teach these skills.

Let's take the case of Muriel and Devon. They were having the above argument in the girls' rest room before school when one of the teachers came in to investigate the disruption.

"Before you girls start throwing punches," Ms. Quincy said, "I'd like to suggest that you let a couple of conflict managers help you work through this."

"Conflict managers?" Muriel said. "What's that?"

"We call them conflict managers here—other schools refer to them as mediators. Whatever you call them, they're here to help you find a solution. They have nothing to do with punishment or discipline. I won't force you to see them—in fact, if you don't both agree that you want to use them, they won't help you." Ms. Quincy crossed her arms and leaned back on the sink. "But I strongly suggest you give it a try, or you're going to end up getting hurt and suspended—and you won't have solved a thing. Are you both up for it?"

Devon and Muriel nodded slowly. They were asked to report to the conference room next to the library during lunch.

Walking into the room, both girls were surprised to find Marita, one of the mediators, setting a pizza on the table.

"Not all programs do this," she said. "We do it here because it keeps people's minds on their problems and off their stomachs."

Devon wasn't surprised to see Marita as a peer mediator. She was an "A" student, on the varsity field hockey team, and never in trouble. But Devon was shocked to see Skye Wassen—who didn't usually get involved in school activities—opening up four colas.

As they all sat down, the door opened and the drama teacher, Mr. Singer, walked in. Muriel and Devon stiffened in their chairs.

"I thought you said we weren't in trouble," Muriel said. "He's a teacher."

"He's cool," Skye said. "He's only here because we've had some people get rough with each other in the past. He won't help with the mediation."

"Right," Devon said.

"Before we begin, I'll explain the ground rules that you both have to follow," Skye said.

"If you feel like you can't follow them, you're allowed to stop right now and leave," Marita said.

"We're here to try to solve the problem," Skye said, "not put blame on anybody."

"No name-calling, foul language, or rude hand signals are allowed," Marita said. She and Skye continued stating the rules.

Students listen to each other as they work toward a solution.

"And finally, we need confidentiality. What you hear and say here, stays here when you leave. After this session, all our notes will be thrown away and the only piece of evidence will be the agreement you sign," Skye said. He and Marita went on to explain the list of rules that they as mediators are required to follow to make sure that a fair solution is created. After hearing the guidelines, Muriel and Devon both agreed to give it a try.

"Then let's start with you," Marita said to Muriel. "Please tell us your side of the story and how the whole situation makes you feel—and remember, Devon, you aren't allowed to interrupt, because your turn is coming."

Explaining your viewpoint is an important step in peer mediation.

Muriel sat back in her chair and started to talk. It was a little hard at first, but Marita and Skye listened so closely that she started to relax.

She explained how she had felt inferior to Devon ever since elementary school. It seemed that everything she wanted and worked hard for, Devon got. Devon made cheerleader, Muriel was cut. Devon had expensive clothes, she didn't. Devon got a job at Shopko, she was turned down. The final straw was when Devon began flirting with the guy Muriel liked. Muriel couldn't believe that Devon was going to get him too—especially when Devon didn't even like him. Muriel was hurt and frustrated so she decided to get Devon where it would hurt—her reputation. She started rumors about Devon.

"She was hurting me, so I hurt her," Muriel said, ending her story.

"Is it my turn now?" Devon asked.

"Not yet," Marita said. "So in this situation, Muriel, you saw that Devon was going after the guy you wanted and so you started spreading rumors about her."

"True rumors," Muriel pointed out.

"How do you feel right now?"

Muriel frowned. "I'm mad."

"You said you were hurt too," Skye said.

"Yeah, when I get hurt I get mad."

Skye gave the sign to Devon to tell the situation as she saw it.

Devon leaned across the table, "You are a liar, Muriel!"

Skye made a buzzing sound with his lips. "Penalty, Devon," he said. "No name-calling. Just tell your story."

Devon sighed. She said that Muriel was right about one thing: they had never gotten along. She didn't know Muriel as a person. But through her friends, she would hear that Muriel was jealous of her. This year, Devon finally got sick of the imagined rivalry. When one of her friends told her that Muriel liked Travis, who also worked at Shopko, she decided to flirt with him. She never dreamed Travis would respond. However she was mad at Muriel for being so petty and jealous for so many years.

"If she can't get the guy she wants, that isn't my fault," Devon said.

"We're not placing blame on anybody, so there's no fault involved," Marita said. *"Let's see if we have your story straight. You didn't like it when Muriel acted jealous for what you thought was no reason, so basically you gave her a reason."*

"Yeah—I like how you put that," Devon said.

"So how do you feel about it?" Skye said.

"I'm mad, too," Devon said, *"that she said mean things about me."*

"Do you feel pleased that you got the result you wanted?" Marita said. *"You wanted to make her mad and take away Travis—and it worked."*

"It seems kind of lame now," Devon said. Muriel looked at Devon in surprise. Finally both girls had stopped blaming the other, started listening, and seemed ready to look for a solution.

"What do you mean?" Marita said.

"I used Travis to get to her and now I'm stuck with him. Besides, I don't want to fight her—I've never been in a fight before."

"Muriel," Skye said. *"Can you think of anything you could have done differently—or maybe that you wish you'd done differently now?"*

"I wish I hadn't told people I wanted to fight her," she blurted out. *"But I was just so sick of always being second."*

"How about you, Devon?" he said.

"I shouldn't have used Travis. It wasn't fair to him."

There was silence for a minute.

"So what now?" Devon said. "We can't change it."

"You can't change the past but you can change the present," Skye said. "What could you do right now, Muriel, to help solve the problem?"

"I already said I was going to fight her, but I guess I could change my mind. I don't want to fight her— I'm not really that mad anymore."

Muriel and Devon, with the help of Marita and Skye, continued to talk. They worked out a solution that both students seemed to like. Devon agreed to stop flirting with Travis. In exchange, Muriel agreed to confront Devon with any angry feelings— face-to-face—and stop spreading rumors to their classmates.

"It sounds like we might have a solution," Skye said. "How does it sound to you both?" Marita read back the agreement.

"Do either of you feel like the other person is taking all the responsibility for the solution?" Marita said.

"Does that matter?" Devon asked.

"Yeah—we want it to be fair to both of you."

Muriel started to make a face and then changed her mind. "Yeah, I can live with it," she said.

"So can I," said Devon.

"Now, you both need to sign the agreement," Marita said. "People seem to stick to things more if it is written and they've signed their name to it."

Talking through the conflict in a peaceful environment helps both people arrive at a solution.

"If anybody breaks it," Skye said, "we get back together and figure out what went wrong."

"Don't expect us to be best friends now," Devon said.

"We don't. We just expect you to honor the agreement."

That is how peer mediation works. But this did not all come easily. Both Marita and Skye spent a lot of time learning the listening and mediating skills that they used.

Peer mediation provides a safe situation in which to work out conflicts. Mediators do not solve the problem, nor do they find a solution. Their only goal is to use mediation techniques they have been taught to help guide the students toward their resolution.

Ground Rules for Fair Play

In order for a resolution to happen in a peaceful way, a few guidelines must be established. The mediators help enforce these guidelines so that all the involved parties are treated fairly. Some guidelines are established for the "arguers." Others are made for the mediators. Let's look at a few:

Rules for the Arguers:

1. Tell the truth.
2. No interrupting.
3. No name-calling, insults, foul language, or rude hand signals.
4. Everything heard during the mediation process is strictly confidential.

Rules for the Mediators:

1. Forcing a solution is prohibited.
2. Everything heard during the mediation process is strictly confidential.
3. Impartiality is required: no judging or taking sides.
4. Help people in conflict listen to each other.

Each rule is very important. It maintains a fair and peaceful environment. The arguers are informed of, and must agree to, the ground rules before the mediation process begins. If the arguers feel that they cannot follow these rules, then the mediators suggest that the mediation not continue. The mediators are informed of the ground rules that they must follow during their required training as well. They also must agree to follow the rules.

Step-by-Step

Each mediation session follows a basic outline or format. There are certain steps that help keep the mediation running smoothly. A usual mediation would be led much like this:

1. Some member of the school, student or faculty, refers the disputing parties to the peer mediation program.
2. The parties are asked if they want a mediator to help solve their problem. If they don't want help or come in expecting everything to be done for them, it won't work.
3. The mediators (there are usually two), the two parties, and an adult go to a neutral place away from other students. Programs try to account for cultural differences by making sure that all the ethnic groups in the school are represented by the mediators.
4. Mediators present the ground rules and everyone agrees to follow them.
5. The first party is asked to explain the conflict. When he or she has told the story, one of the mediators paraphrases, or restates, it.

6. The first party is asked how he or she feels.
7. The second party is asked to explain the conflict. When he or she has finished, one of the mediators paraphrases, or restates, it.
8. The second party is asked how he or she feels. Steps 5 through 8 are done to help both sides listen to, and understand, each other. It is impossible to reach a fair solution together without that understanding.
9. The first person is asked what he or she could have done differently. One of the mediators paraphrases the answer.
10. The second person is asked what he or she could have done differently. One of the mediators paraphrases the answer.
11. The first person is asked what he or she could do right now to help solve the problem. One of the mediators paraphrases the answer.
12. The second person is asked what he or she could do right now to help solve the problem. One of the mediators paraphrases the answer.
13. The mediators ask creative questions to bring the two parties closer to a specific and fair solution. The best solution is one with which both parties are comfortable.
14. One mediator reads the solution out loud and asks if both parties agree.
15. If both parties agree, they sign the agreement. They now "own" the solution, because they have come up with it themselves.

16. If they can't reach an agreement, the two par-
    ties either agree to disagree peacefully or are
    referred to someone else who might be able to
    help them work out their problems.

   Peer mediation works best when it follows these
guidelines. The structure allows the participants to
have a fair discussion of the conflict. No one is
insulted, or made to feel bad. Both people are giv-
en a fair chance to describe the situation as they
see it. Both people are given a fair and equal
chance to respond.
   A good way to gauge a school program's success is through the students. Here are reported
changes noticed by peer mediators around the
country:

• Students are initiating contact with mediators,
  without the interference of a faculty member.
• Teachers and faculty are more accepting of peer
  mediation as an alternative (and more perma-
  nent!) method of resolving student conflicts.
• More and more students are viewing mediation
  as a safe place to take problems they wouldn't
  share with a parent, teacher, or principal.

   People feel good when they have worked hard
to solve their own problems. Peer mediation gives
them a chance to look at the problem from a different angle.

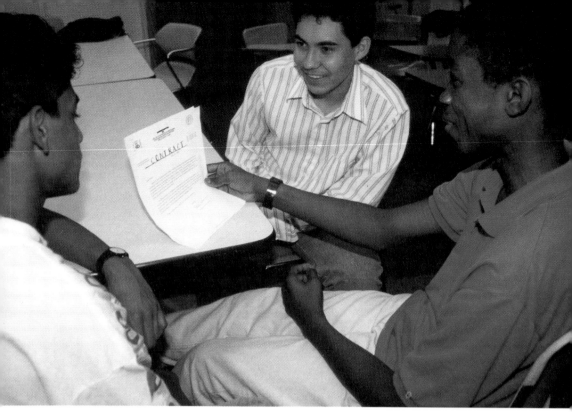

The solution to the conflict is written down and signed by both people.

It also presents a situation in which both parties can "win." The agreement is reached by both students. No one feels like a coward, and no one has a black eye!

Chapter 3

Choosing Peer Mediation

*I*t all started when Angel told Darrell she had seen his girlfriend out with another guy on Saturday night. He called her a liar and insulted her skin color. She threatened to get him if he didn't apologize. He warned that if she kept insulting his girlfriend, his "family" would take care of her.

By lunchtime, Angel and Darrell were calling fellow gang members—both inside and outside of school. Before the last bell rang signaling the end of lunch, a mob of curious kids had gathered in front of the school. An argument was on the verge of turning into a bloody gang war.

Rumors of weapons had already floated into the principal's office. The principal broke into the middle of the crowd and pulled Angel and Darrell into his office. They were offered a choice: suspension or peer mediation.

*After an hour of intense discussion with two medi-
ators, Angel and Darrell signed a contract to end
the disagreement and call off their gangs. Only time
would tell whether they would stick to it, but the
principal was confident. Since the peer mediation
program had begun at his school, the suspension
rate had been cut in half.*

Having a peer mediation program doesn't mean
students will never fight or argue again. Conflict is
part of our everyday lives, but with practice, you
can learn the skills to deal with it in a nonviolent
way.

Conflicts will usually dissolve if they are settled
without the "help" of friends. It is the involvement
of others that will often lead to physical violence.
Peer mediation can help solve a wide range of conflicts, from petty theft to harassment by another
student. The important thing to remember is that
small or large, conflict is best resolved in a peaceful and protected environment.

It is also important to remember that there is
often more than one right answer to a problem.
The mediation session encourages the "arguers"
to come to a solution of their own, a compromise
with which they can both live.

Common Conflicts

Peer mediation works best when the dispute is
only between two people. This can include such

Peer mediation only works when both people agree to give it a
chance.

situations as campus fistfights or arguments over campaign tactics during a student government election. Many conflicts arise from name-calling, harassment, and relationship troubles. Other big issues are gossip and rumors. Those are the kinds of conflicts that peer mediators can help resolve.

Because of peer pressure, pride, and other factors, conflicts arising from hurtful gossip and rumors are often solved violently. Peer mediation provides a more peaceful, honest approach to solving conflicts. Following is a list of some common reasons behind conflicts, provided by students involved in mediation programs:

- bullying
- classism (rich vs. poor)
- disputes on the athletic field
- disrespect
- ending of friendships or relationships
- jealousy
- misunderstandings
- personal property
- racism
- sexism

Basically, a good peer mediation program will deal with any issue in which both parties are willing to give it a chance. However, as we mentioned earlier in the "ground rules," both people need to agree that they want to work out a solution. Without their cooperation, it won't work.

Seriously violent conflicts pose a threat to the peer mediators and other school members. These conflicts need tougher discipline measures than peer mediation.

Danger: Out-of-Reach

It is important to remember that not every type of conflict can be settled through peer mediation. In fact, there are some situations that peer mediators are advised *not* to handle.

Experts in peer mediation agree that certain issues need to be brought before school officials or other adults. Peer mediators should not be put into a position where they have to deal with them. These issues include serious violence or abuse, weapons, illegal activities, and other large issues of injustice.

So, the program *won't* be used to mediate for a student seeking help because he got shortchanged on a drug deal. A girl who is being abused by her boyfriend will be referred to a counseling center, not the mediation room. And for a student showing up in gym class with a knife, the police will be called in, not the mediation team.

Conflict resolution programs, such as peer mediation, do not take the place of tough discipline codes for violent or troubled students. Schools still need to do everything within their power to provide a safe environment. While peer mediation can be a part of that, it won't take care of all the problems.

Peer mediators know that when serious problems arise during a mediation, they are not to try to handle them by themselves. For instance, if a student talks about suicide during a session, the peer mediator is not required to keep that confidential. He or she should report it to a staff adviser immediately. If a student seems excessively troubled, the peer mediator should alert a counselor or school psychologist. Of course, if someone makes a violent threat during the mediation, the discussion stops and the necessary adults are called in.

Peer mediators are not experts. They can't handle every problem that comes along. They are, however, skilled in resolving the everyday conflicts that we all face.

Peer mediators help people deal with anger, communicate feelings, respect differences, find a common ground, and facilitate solutions in which everybody wins.

Chapter 4

Peer Mediators in Training

Unfortunately, it sometimes takes a shocking event to convince students that peer mediation can work for them. That's what happened to students at Bronx Regional High School in New York City.

When a student was murdered by a classmate, the other students suddenly realized that they were going to have to help each other stay alive. They saw the recently created peer mediation program as one possible step to a less violent school. One student admits, "Not everything is going to be solved when you mediate a dispute. What's important is that you make the effort."

Don't be fooled. The peer mediators you've read about so far in this book were not born knowing how to help people solve conflicts. They had to learn the skills that it takes to be a good conflict manager.

Choosing Peer Mediators

Most schools ask the student body to suggest students who will make good mediators. In other schools, a Mediation Committee interviews and selects candidates for the training program.

The best mediating programs contain mediators from diverse racial, religious, and economic backgrounds. Not all mediators should be National Honor Society members, student government officers, or varsity athletes. The best mediator is a student who possesses natural charm, sincerity, and a caring nature.

Peer mediation programs need a wide range of individuals to act as mediators. Each mediator brings with him or her a deep knowledge of a specialized group. For instance, Denise is Asian American and is a member of the National Honor Society, while Nick, a Native American, is in the drama club. Marita is an athlete of Hispanic descent, and Skye doesn't belong to any official school group. When he was given responsibility within the system, he seemed to understand students who felt out of place. His status helped him help others solve their conflicts.

As one peer mediator said, "You need nerds, jocks, preppies, punks . . . ."

Once a student has been nominated for the program, he or she must decide whether it is a good personal choice. Following is a list of

Peer mediators come from all backgrounds.

It is very important for peer mediators to relate well with other people.

some questions that might help a prospective mediator take a good look at the many issues involved.

- Am I a good communicator? Do I listen carefully when people talk? Am I clearly understood when I talk?
- Can I empathize with people?
- Can I keep secrets? Do I respect the need for privacy and confidentiality?
- Am I a leader or do people feel they can rely on me?
- Am I successful at solving my own conflicts with people?
- Am I cooperative? A good team player?
- Do I care about stopping violence?

Peer Mediation Training Program

There are several different groups around the country who train mediators. While some aspects of the training program vary from group to group, they all share a similar goal.

Each program requires the trainee to spend a certain number of hours—ranging in length from sixteen to twenty—in group sessions learning the basic skills of peer mediation. After this initial training, ten more hours of follow-up instruction are also required.

Training sessions are run by conflict resolution professionals. Trainees are taught the

interpersonal and conflict resolution skills they will
need to help other students settle conflicts.

Mediators About Mediating

Marita begins, "The first thing they teach you is
the definition of conflict. There are different types,
and different ways of communicating. You have to
understand this first before you go into the process itself."

Nick adds, "I was blown away at first by how
often everybody interrupted each other—including
me! We had to learn to listen. Then we practiced
seeing both sides and staying calm when things
get ugly. . . . It can really get emotional in a mediating session. I wouldn't have known how to deal
with that without the training."

"I remember," says Denise, "that they trained us
to listen to what somebody said and then repeat
that back in our own words. It seemed lame at
first, but it really works. Every one of the mediators in my group was good at something. One guy
was good at reflecting back feelings. Somebody
else was good at restating what someone said. I've
found that I am really best at clearing away all the
garbage and getting to the heart of the matter.
These are all skills that a good mediator needs."

Skye says, "What I really liked is when we were
involved in the activities. You don't just sit around
and listen to people tell you what conflict is: you
get up and do things. For example, they'd give us

Role-playing introduces peer mediators to many of the issues that they may face in their mediation sessions.

a mini-lecture, and then we would role-play a mediation. After, we would all discuss it, usually in groups of three or four. Every time we got into those groups, we had to practice active listening, which is where one person has a minute to talk and everybody else has to listen without interrupting. We'd have a chance to say, 'Now let me make sure I understand what you said,' so then the person listening explains what they heard the other person say. And the person speaking gets to say, 'No, this part is right, but that part is wrong.' For me that was cool, because it was probably the first time I ever got to talk in my life without anyone interrupting me."

"I liked the activities too," Denise says. "We didn't just role-play—we interviewed each other. We did a lot of group dialogue and brainstorming. You had to take part in every activity or you didn't learn. It really taught me how to express my feelings better and see both sides of an argument."

Skye grins. "I had to learn to cooperate, which is hard for me. But I learned I could really spot prejudice when it came up and I *wasn't* afraid to interrupt that!"

"In my training," Nick says, "we used art projects and mime—where you have to draw or act out an emotion without using words. That helped me learn to see how people are feeling, even when they're not saying it."

"They had some neat ways of showing us messages," Denise remembers. "There was one lesson called the 'Torn Heart.' They had this big red paper heart symbolizing somebody's self-esteem. They had me walk the heart through the group. The other people played the roles of people at school, saying things to me as I walked by. Every time I heard something negative, I'd tear away a piece of the heart. By the end of the exercise, I had only a small ripped piece of my heart left. It made us realize that the more people are put-down, the smaller their self-esteem becomes. That's why there's the rule about no put-downs in mediation."

Marita says, "The thing that has helped me the most is when they'd present us with a conflict. We acted just like it was a real mediation, and then we'd all brainstorm for solutions. Now the questions I ask to get kids to come up with their resolutions just come naturally to me."

There are other important aspects of peer mediation training. Most trainers include the following lessons and activities:

- Meeting in a circle so everyone can participate.
- Giving everyone the right to pass on any activity until they feel comfortable.
- Announcing what is going to happen at the beginning of every session and asking the students how it sounds to them, so they feel empowered and involved.
- Taking stock of each session at the end and using the results to plan for the next session.
- Practicing what you preach. Trainers try to use good communication skills, cooperation, and conflict resolution—all the things they're teaching—so the students can see it in action.

Follow-Up Training

Once peer mediators begin to work in their school, questions and problems usually arise that were not addressed in training. Follow-up sessions, run by trainers, give mediators a chance to have their questions answered. Some of the more common issues include:

Mediation training gives students a chance to try out conflict resolution techniques.

- Being aware of their own biases and staying neutral.
- Seeing how cultural differences affect the way people think and deal with conflict.
- Realizing how power issues can affect all of the people involved, even mediators.

Ongoing Training

Training never ends for peer mediators. They are always learning "on the job," and they have chances to share new ideas with each other and with their adult advisers.

In some programs, there is a box at the bottom of the mediation report form labeled "I Need to

Talk." If the mediator checks that, the advisers know that student has something he or she would like to debrief. Debriefing means discussing something after it happens to try to make sense out of it.

Take the Initiative

Now you have seen many different situations where peer mediation has made a difference. Peer mediation programs exist at many schools across the country, but they are not yet everywhere. If you want to start a program in your school, these suggestions might be helpful to you. Obviously you can't do it alone, but you can get things started.

1. There are several organizations you can write to or call for information. See the Where to Go for Help section located at the end of this book.
2. Take that information to a teacher or administrator you know is interested in creative ways to stop conflict and violence in your school. The best programs, the experts say, start with the staff. Without their support, it will never get off the ground.
3. Ask to be included in the planning. The experts also say that the most successful programs make good use of student ideas and energy.
4. Be willing to help raise money, recruit students who are interested in becoming mediators, and

participate in presentations to school and community groups.

5. Remember that not everyone is going to accept
the idea immediately. If you have all the facts
and you keep your enthusiasm fired-up, you can
persuade some people to support a mediation
program. Others will have to see it working
before they are won over.

If you do try to start a peer mediation program,
you will be doing your part to help lower violence
at your school. Conflict will always be present, but
there are good ways to resolve it before it gets
destructive.

Chapter 5

Valuable Skills

It can cost up to $10,000 for a school to run a peer mediation program.

This money could also buy new books, computers, or sports equipment. Why would a school spend that much money to settle arguments between students?

The answer lies in the fact that peer mediation does more than help solve individual romantic and after-school squabbles. No one learns well when they're worried about fistfights over parking spaces, violence in the cafeteria, or harassment on the school bus. Without a safe atmosphere, your education will suffer. Mediation programs benefit the entire student body—and can even help the community. Plus, skills learned in school will also help later in life.

Groups, such as the Community Board Program (CBP) and NAME, have come up with the following

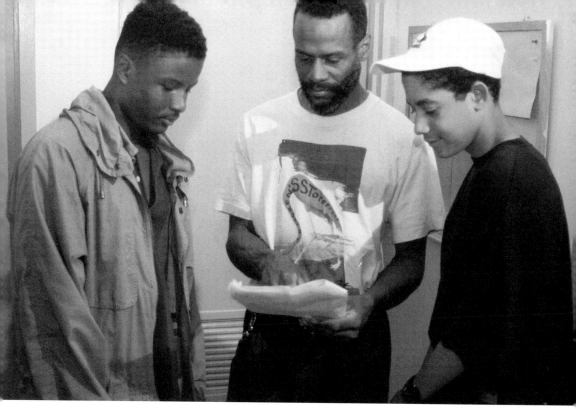

Peer mediators learn many skills that will help them in their daily lives.

list of ways that mediation training and experience help peer mediators:

- Increased confidence and self-esteem.
- Improved academics.
- Better relationships at home, in school, and in sports.
- Positive role models for other students.
- Better understanding of other people and themselves.
- Increased interest in justice and the American legal system.

Peace in Our Schools

If the fear and danger of violence can be lessened in your school, the climate changes and it becomes much easier to learn. Becoming involved with peer mediation is one positive step that you can take to try and make your school safe. Schools with mediation programs report a reduction in violence, fighting, tension, and vandalism; reduced number of suspensions for conflict; better relations between students and teachers; decreased absences; improved academics, critical thinking, and problem-solving; better relations between the school and parents; more time spent by teachers on teaching and less on discipline.

As one expert has said, if everyone tries to live by the skills and philosophy of conflict resolution, the program becomes part of the way the school runs. Here is one real-life example of peer mediation making a difference in the level of violence in American schools:

In the fall of 1988, at the Washington Middle School in Albuquerque, New Mexico, the school administration decided to try using conflict resolution to end the gang violence in its school.

Two mediation organizations helped them set up a program. They persuaded the leaders of three major gangs to meet for two hours, twice a week. The gang leaders discussed all of their issues, from the safety of their families to the way the administration treated them.

At the end of a month, the gang leaders and the school's principal signed an agreement. They agreed that threats and name-calling would stop and gang members would try to settle future disputes peacefully. The fighting among the rival gangs soon ended, and they have continued to hold mediation sessions. They learned that conflicts can be resolved without violence.

Beyond the School Walls

The results of a study completed for the Academy of Family Mediators (AFM) confirm what many people believed to be true: students involved in peer mediation programs in school take home the skills that they have learned.

Those involved in the study documented a strong decrease in how often and how violently the kids in the family fought when they were participating in peer mediation at school. Kids are using better communication skills and parents have to interfere less often. Conflict resolution skills seem to continue working long after the school day is over.

Peer Mediators Speak Out

The benefits of peer mediation affect not only the "arguers" but the mediators as well. Mediators often benefit from their training in many other parts of their lives. Here are a few of their stories:

Peer mediation helps people improve their listening skills.

The valuable skills gained through mediation sessions will help you peaceably deal with conflicts for the rest of your life.

Stephen: I used to skip school a lot. Being a peer mediator gives me a reason to go to school and a sense of importance when I get there.

Carolyn: Before I became a peer mediator, I was even too shy to answer questions in class. I've gained confidence from this program—now you can't shut me up!

Tiffany: It has given me a positive outlook on life. I know how to communicate well, and without that, all the education in the world won't help you.

Joel: It's shown me that if you look at all the violence in society you could get pretty depressed. But if you take one situation at a time, you can make a difference.

A Vision of Peace

Peer mediation encourages people to listen to one another when there are problems. It shows people that they can work toward peaceable solutions with the information they share. It shows people how to accomplish this by helping them work through problem situations when they arise.

"Learning to deal with conflict is a lifelong gift," says Sister Noel Marra, Director of the Cleveland Mediation Center. The skills that you learn from mediation can be applied to situations far beyond the school walls. Conflict is a part of life, and those who learn to deal with it peacefully are far ahead of everyone else.

The groups and individuals mentioned in this book, along with thousands of other people, believe that we can turn back the tide of violence. And young people provide both fresh ideas and open minds. As the great peacemaker Mahatma Gandhi once said, "If we are to reach real peace in this world . . . we shall have to begin with the children."

Through peer mediation or conflict resolution, you can help change the world—one conflict at a time.

Glossary—*Explaining New Words*

active listening   The act of listening to one person talk at a time without interruption.

biases   Beliefs that sway your thinking and make you prejudiced.

confidentiality   Something private or secret.

conflict managers   Students who listen to a conflict and, using their training, help their peers arrive at a solution they can live with.

conflict resolution movement   A movement dedicated to finding ways to solve problems without physical or verbal force which arose out of the 1960s peace movement.

debrief   To discuss something after it happens in an attempt to try and make sense out of it and learn from it.

empathize   To understand or be sensitive to the thoughts, feelings, or experiences of someone else.

empowered   To take control of your life and have a say in what happens to you.

facilitate To help or assist someone reach a goal.

impartiality Not having a preference for either side of an argument.

inferior Feeling less important.

mediate The act of helping people settle their differences.

participants People who take part or are involved in an activity (in this case the peer mediation).

peaceable school A safe school where students can try peaceful ways to resolve their conflicts when the problems are still minor.

peer mediation A conflict resolution program in which students mediate conflicts between other students using a structured process.

prohibited Forbidden.

prejudice An opinion formed without taking the time to judge fairly.

rivalry A competition or a feeling of competitiveness between two or more people.

self-esteem Feeling of confidence in yourself.

Where to Go for Help

Children's Creative
  Response to Conflict
  Program (CCRC)
Fellowship of
  Reconciliation
Box 271
Nyack, NY 10960
(914)358-4924

Cleveland Mediation
  Center
Community Based Youth
  Mediation Program
3000 Bridge Avenue
Cleveland, OH 44113
(216)771-7297
e-mail: djoyce@igc.apc.org

Community Board
  Program (CBP)
1540 Market Street
Suite 490
San Francisco, CA 94102
(415)552-1250
e-mail: cmbrds@conflict-
  net.org

Educators for Social
  Responsibility
School Conflict Resolution
  Programs
23 Garden Street
Cambridge, MA 02138
(617)492-1764
e-mail: esrmain@igc.
  apc.org
Web site: http://www.ben-
  jerry.com

Illinois Institute for
  Dispute Resolution
110 W. Main Street
Urbana, IL 61801
(217)384-4118
e-mail: iidr@aol.com

National Association for
  Mediation in Education
  (NAME)
425 Smith Street
Amherst, MA 01002
(413)545-2462

Resolving Conflicts
  Creatively Program
  (RCCP)
163 Third Avenue, #103
New York, NY 10003
(212)387-0225
e-mail: rccp@igr.apc.org
  or esrrccp@aol.com
Web site: http://www.ben-
  jerry.com

Ohio Commission on
  Dispute Resolution
77 South High Street,
  24th Floor
Columbus, OH 43266-
  0124
(614)752-9595
e-mail:
  ocdrcm@igc.apc.org

For Further Reading

Carter, Jimmy. *Talking Peace*. New York: Dutton Children's Books, 1993.

Dehr, Roma; Ronald Bazar; and Dorothy Morrison. *We Can Do It!* Vancouver, British Columbia: Namchi United Enterprises, 1985.

Fisher, Roger, and William Ury. *Getting to Yes: Negotiating Agreement Without Giving In*. New York: Penguin Books, 1983.

Klee, Shelia. *Working Together Against School Violence*. New York: Rosen Publishing Group, Inc, 1996.

Nathan, Amy. *Everything You Need to Know About Conflict Resolution*. New York: Rosen Publishing Group, Inc, 1996.

Sorenson, D. L. *Conflict Resolution and Mediation for Peer Helpers*. Minneapolis, MN: Educational Media Corporation, 1992.

Terrell, Ruth Harris. *A Kid's Guide to How to Stop the Violence*. New York: Avon Books, 1992.

Ury, William. *Getting Past No: Negotiating with Difficult People*. New York: Bantam Books. 1991.

Weeks, Dudley. *The Eight Essential Steps to Conflict Resolution*. New York: G. P. Putnam's Sons, 1992.

Index

A
abuse, 37
Academy of Family
    Mediators (AFM), 54
anger, 11–12, 14, 19, 25, 38
anxiety, 14

B
Bronx Regional High
    School, 39

C
Cleveland Mediation Center,
    56
communication, 12, 38, 43,
    54
Community Board Program
    (CBP), 51–52
confidentiality, 21, 27, 38, 43
conflict, 11, 33–35, 58
    reasons for, 35
conflict managers, 19, 39–43
conflict resolution, 54
    definition, 7
    history of, 12–13
    leading to peaceful
        solutions, 12, 15–16,
        24–27, 31, 53–54
    programs, 37–38
counselors, 37–38

D
Department of Justice, 13
detention, 14
drugs, 37

E
Educators for Social
    Responsibility, 18

F
fighting, 11, 18–19, 23–25,
    33, 53

G
Gandhi, Mahatma, 58
gang violence, 32–33, 53–54
gossip, 35
ground rules for fair play,
    27–28
guns and weapons, 13, 32,
    37

L
listening to others, 12, 24,
    26–27, 43–45

M
Marra, Sister Noel, 56–58
mediation, 11, 14–17,
    19–21
    training for, 26–27, 39–50,
    52
murder, 39

N
name-calling, 20, 23, 27, 35,
    54
National Association for
    Mediation in Education
    (NAME), 18, 51–52

choosing to use, 32–38
definition, 6–7
when it doesn't work,
    37–38
peer mediation programs,
    11–12, 17, 18, 39
  costs of starting, 51
  examples of, 14–16,
    18–26, 32–33, 53
  process for, 28–30
  reasons for success,
    13–14, 30–31
  rules of, 15, 18–31
  signing agreements,
    16–17, 25–26, 29,
    54
  typical results, 53
peer pressure, 35
prejudice, 11, 46
pride, 11, 35

R
rivalry, 23
rumors, 22–23, 25, 32, 35

S
schools, 17, 37, 53–54
  crime in, 13, 39
self-esteem, 46, 52
situations, 6, 14–16, 18–26,
    32–33

V
vandalism, 53
violence
  alternatives to, 7, 11–12,
    33, 54
  in homes, 7
  in schools, 7–9, 12–13, 17
  reasons for, 18–19, 33, 35

W
Washington Middle School,
    53

About the Author
Nancy Rue has written three previous books on youth social issues. She has worked with teenagers for twenty-two years as a teacher, theater director, and youth group leader. She lives with her husband and daughter in Nevada.

Photo Credits
Cover photo by Michael Brandt; Photographs on pages 55, 56 by Kim Sonsky/Matthew Baumann; all other photos by Ira Fox.